How to be (a little bit) GREEK

STAVROS FLATLEY

TRANSWORLD PUBLISHERS
61–63 Uxbridge Road, London W5 5SA
A Random House Group Company
www.rbooks.co.uk

First published in Great Britain
in 2009 by Bantam Press
an imprint of Transworld Publishers

Thanks to Carlsberg and Saatchi & Saatchi for permission
to pay special homage to their advertising.

Editorial director: Sarah Emsley
Design by Lynnette Eve / www.design-jam.co.uk
Photography by Robin Matthews
Edited by Mari Roberts

A CIP catalogue record for this book
is available from the British Library.

ISBN 9780593065549

Addresses for Random House Group Ltd companies outside the UK
can be found at: www.randomhouse.co.uk
The Random House Group Ltd Reg. No. 954009

The Random House Group Limited supports The Forest Stewardship
Council (FSC), the leading international forest-certification organization.
All our titles that are printed on Greenpeace-approved FSC-certified paper carry
the FSC logo. Our paper procurement policy can be found at
www.rbooks.co.uk/environment

Printed and bound in Great Britain by
Butler Tanner & Dennis Ltd, Frome

2 4 6 8 10 9 7 5 3 1

CONTENTS

How to be (a little bit) GREEK

STAVROS FLATLEY

BANTAM PRESS

LONDON · NEW YORK · TORONTO · SYDNEY · AUCKLAND

INTRODUCTION

As Simon Cowell would be the first to admit, no one can be that cool without being (a little bit) Greek.

History is stuffed full of inspirational Greeks. Simons, Anthonys and Georges by the score. Archimedes, obviously. Zeus. Winston Churchill.[1] Barack Obama.[2] Brad Pitt. Papou.[3] Zorba the Greek.

Some people miss the boat altogether. Sir Walter Raleigh, for example. He could so easily have been a little bit Greek if instead of bringing back a shipload of potatoes with the tobacco, he'd stuffed the hold with fake onyx ashtrays and gold-lacquered replicas of the Statue of Liberty.

Queen Victoria was another. She could have had the honour of being Britain's first Greek royal if instead of saying 'We are not amused' the whole time and pulling a face like she was sucking a lemon, she'd flung a bit of crockery around after dinner and produced a Full English for Albert and his mates when they'd taken a break from the poker table at three o'clock in the morning.

---

[1] When the Greeks defeated the Italian fascists in 1941, Churchill fired up a King Edward Invincible and said, 'We will not say thereafter that the Greeks fight like heroes, but heroes fight like the Greeks.'

[2] From the moment he said, 'Yes, we can!'

[3] My granddad.

INTRODUCTION

For Scott of the Antarctic, it was close, but no cigar. He could have gone down in history as (a little bit) Greek if instead of moaning about the cold he'd fired up the BBQ and served the last of the corned beef as kebabs.

Captain Oates, on the other hand, was well Greek. 'I'm going out now, and I may be some time,' was his immortal quote, and it's one I've used on more than one occasion down the years.

As for solo explorers, solo sailors, solo anybody – what's the point of doing it if you can't share the after-show party? Climb Everest if you will, but don't limit the fun on the summit to you and Sherpa Tenzing. I'm up for it, and so's my Greek mate Mick – and half of Cockfosters will be too once they get wind my wife's getting busy with the primus.

How Greek Are You?

Anybody who saves Christmas wrapping paper and bits of string is definitely not Greek. The only thing a Greek saves is money – and only so he can pin it to his daughter's wedding dress, not just have it swiped by the Inland Revenue. Giving, not taking – that's what it's all about.

I know I promised on the jacket to teach you *How to be (a little bit) Greek*, but the truth is, there are no half measures. You've got to be fully committed. You can't just leave the wedding on the Monday morning. You've got to throw the extra plate, dance the extra jig, polish off that last tray of *baklava.*

Here's a little test: did you only buy one copy of this book? *What? You did? ONLY ONE?* I've got to be honest with you – it's not looking good from where I'm standing. But we all make mistakes. There's still time. Go and buy ten more, so all your mates can have one. No mates? Don't worry. I can help you there too.

How to be (a little bit) Greek might not look like much, but as Ant and Dec have shown us, appearances can be deceptive. This book is THE BUSINESS. It's packed full of timeless wisdom from a lifetime at the head of the dinner table, in the *taverna* and on the dancefloor. It will draw from a rich fund of personal anecdotes – not just from me, but from my granddad, my nan (a very wise old girl), and Lagi, my son, who's taught me a good few moves of his own.

Welcome – *parakalo!* – and let's serve the starters.

Stavros Flatley
Cockfosters, August 2009

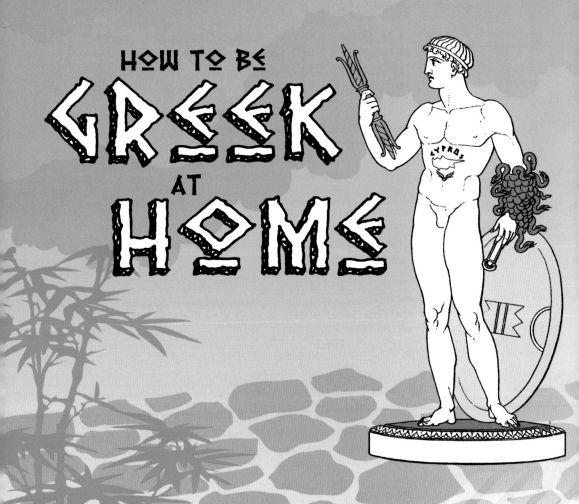

HOW TO BE GREEK AT HOME

(a little bit)

HOW TO BE GREEK . . .
AT HOME

Some people are born with a flair for home decor, but even if you're one of them, I've got to be honest with you – you'll be struggling to keep up with the Greek way of doing things.

You see, being a little bit Greek – even a teensy-weensy *iota* Greek – doesn't end when you come home in the evening, shut the Corinthian-column-enhanced front door behind you and announce to your wife that you're ready for dinner. It's an all-embracing lifestyle – and that means your home must be a true reflection of who and what you are.

Imagine inviting a few friends back to your place after an all-night poker game and waiting for your wife to rustle up a Full English. Would you want to be surrounded by white walls, sanded floorboards, colour-coordinated scatter cushions, a minimalist fireplace and no mantelpiece? You're right – it doesn't bear thinking about.

As a beginner, you'll want to know how to make your home look the part without a lifetime's experience of being Greek. It can seem pretty daunting. If you haven't had my grandparents as your style gurus, how do you know what is and isn't acceptable? It isn't as if you can just grab a copy of *Ideal Greek* down the newsagents and hit the ground running.

That's where this book comes to your aid – and here is the first of many secrets I'm going to share with you: *it's not rocket science* (even though the Greeks invented the rocket). If you want to be a little bit Greek at home (and who doesn't?), you should start by concentrating on two major areas:

- the mantelpiece, and

- the BBQ.

Going the Full Donkey

Whilst a novice might be tempted to adorn the mantelpiece with an antique alabaster bust of a composer

HOW TO BE GREEK AT HOME

> *Show me a man's mantelpiece and I'll tell you the story of his life*

or philosopher, a Greek knows instinctively that only gold lacquer and fake onyx will do. When it comes to decoration, there's no room for half measures. Have the courage of your convictions. Where a Brit might be tempted by a glass donkey with a small brass-effect bell, you mustn't hold back. Bring home the one with a thermometer on its back, hauling a miniature golf-caddy laden with club-shaped drinks stirrers. The magic word you're looking for here is *overkill*.

Most people have a bit of a weakness for an ornament, but only Greeks buy them by the porcelain-wishing-well bucketload. When we played with my granddad's collection as kids, he was always shouting, 'Hey, be careful with that – that'll be worth a lot of money one day.' You'd have thought we were messing with Ming vases, not a donkey in a sombrero that dispensed cigarettes out of its bum when you lifted its tail.

The British stuff might turn out to be worth a fortune twenty or thirty years down the line, but who wants to wait that long? There's no time like the present for a Greek. You don't see us selling off the family heirlooms, and you never will – well, not until fake onyx makes a comeback.

HOW TO BE GREEK . . .
AT HOME IMPROVEMENTS

(a little bit)

There's very little around the home – his own or somebody else's – that a Greek can't improve. As Archimedes said, 'Give me a lever and a place to stand and I will move the earth.' It's in our nature to make things better for you. We saw the British drink tea and we added a cinnamon stick. We saw the British Museum and we added the Elgin Marbles . . .

The Ancient Greeks were master architects. The Colossus of Rhodes, the Parthenon, the Pyramids, Stonehenge – the ancient Greeks won the contract on every one of the seven wonders of the world. And what's more, they got it done on time and for cash. The only Big One they didn't have a hand in was the Leaning Tower of Pisa. No way would it have leaned if a Greek had built it, unless the architect took his inspiration from the sculpture of a Satyr that has pride of place on Mick's mantelpiece.

HOW TO BE GREEK . . .
ON THE PATIO

(a little bit)

There was a time when no self-respecting Greek would be seen in public without a fleet of oil tankers and cruise liners at his elbow. But nowadays, if there's one arena where a Greek stands head and shoulders above the crowd, it's not on the quayside, it's on the patio – or wherever it is you keep your barbecue. Barbecue has three syllables but it's still too small a word to describe everything that happens from the moment you light the charcoal and flip the tea towel over your shoulder. It should come as no surprise to you, therefore, to learn that we chose to put the whole glorious experience in capitals.

Greeks look at BBQs the way Italians see Ferraris. We want to get the best there is. BBQ envy is not a pretty sight – except when it's aimed in your direction. I've found that six BBQs are just about the right number to own – not including the clay oven. You'll only use two of them, but definitely need the other four. One should have skewers two feet long that can pierce a pig's flesh as easily as a hot knife through butter. They're held over the flame on an enclosed rotating cog set that can gear its speed to the weight of the meat. I haven't tried them yet because they're still in their packaging, but you see where I'm coming from.

BBQ DOS AND DON'TS

- When inviting guests round, the host should always have a new Outdoor Living gadget to show off, or at the very least a shiny set of tongs.

- Always invite at least twenty people. Any fewer and the wife might as well fire up the kitchen oven – and that's no way to impress your guests.

- The charcoal should be lit approximately sixty minutes before cooking commences. This allows plenty of time for the family to admire your ignition technique, as you put a match to the firelighters in a safe yet manly fashion.

HOW TO BE GREEK AT HOME

- Do not under any circumstances use a gas BBQ. This is the coward's way out. A Greek will see it as his duty to ridicule any gas BBQ on sight, except perhaps if it's owned by his bank manager.

- Guests who bring something should be wary, as the size and quality of their offering will be scrutinized and later taken apart. This is the origin of the phrase, 'Beware Greeks bearing gifts.'

- Ladies, feel free to help the woman of the house with the serving of the food and, later, with clearing the table and washing up.

- The BBQ area should be as far away from the house as possible, to fortify the impression that the men are on their own little island.

- Old-fashioned wooden chairs should be provided for the men to sit around the BBQ and recreate the ambience of the village *taverna*. The host might be the richest Greek in London but at times like this he is never far from his roots.

- The men, accompanied from time to time by their sons, and when invited to do so by the host, may pick little bits of meat off the grill. They will tell stories of village life and make jokes about families

from other villages. 'You know why the Spiros don't BBQ? Because the beans fall through the bars . . .'

- It is customary for the host to tell all the best stories. He is the BBQ king and he will hold court around his grill.

- The tea towel is his ceremonial robe, and shall stay over his shoulder until all the guests have left.

- At no time should the host panic. The wife can, but he should stay calm. If things do go disastrously wrong, he should do the manly thing and blame anything – and anyone – other than himself.

The Golden Rules of the BBQ

For those of you who might still be some distance from being (even a little bit) Greek, it's important to spell out the etiquette of this most sublime and Greek of all activities.

When you announce a forthcoming BBQ, it sets in motion a chain of events that onlookers may easily confuse with the preparations for a State Banquet.

First, there's a lot of routine, back-room stuff that needn't bother the man. He is totally focused on the challenge ahead. If you're looking for a role model here, think Russell Crowe in *Gladiator* – but with more skewers.

RULE 1: The wife goes to Tescos and buys all the food except the meat. The man has already primed his friend the butcher.

RULE 2: The wife makes the dips, potato salad, macaroni, meatballs and dessert. She also pops the meat into the marinades (unless she's gone the Granddad route, in which case see page 158–6).

RULE 3: The wife prepares the meat for cooking, places it on a tray along with the necessary cooking utensils and sauces, and takes it to the man who is holding court – whisky in hand – beside the grill.

RULE 4: The wife remains outside the compulsory three-metre exclusion zone where testosterone-charged exuberance and manly bonding activities can take place without interference.

RULE 5: *The man places the meat upon the grill.* (Any attempt to interfere with this part of the ritual will lead to much pushing and shoving and flicking with the tea towel.)

RULE 6: The wife goes inside to assemble the plates and cutlery. She will reappear every so often to gather some freshly cooked meat and to ask if it's time to call the fire brigade. The man will respond with some harmlessly chauvinistic remark. His companions will snigger appreciatively and the wife will hurry off to obey his further commands. She too is caught up in the whole BBQ ritual, and will put up with this behaviour in front of her husband's friends; the unwritten rule of the BBQ stands in any Greek marriage. But she never forgets who stepped on whose foot during the marriage ceremony (see Greek weddings, page 91), and may well employ a brace of skewers and a well-aimed tea towel to remind him of this once the festivities have been concluded.

RULE 7: The wife tells the man that the meat is looking great, and maybe she doesn't need to call the fire brigade after all. He thanks her and asks if she will bring more Coke and ice for his whisky.

RULE 8: *The man takes the meat off the grill and hands it to the wife.*

RULE 9: The wife brings the plates, salad, bread, utensils, napkins and sauces to the table.

RULE 10: After eating, the wife clears the table and does the dishes.

RULE 11: Everyone praises the man's culinary artistry and thanks him for his hospitality.

RULE 12: The men will reach for the whisky once more and sing songs of struggle. These songs will get louder and louder as the evening progresses. No women will be invited to sing. What do they know of struggle? When the guests have left, the man asks the wife how she enjoyed her day off, and, upon seeing her reaction, concludes that there's just no pleasing some women.

HOW TO BE GREEK AT HOME

(a little bit)

HOW TO BE GREEK . . .
ABOUT FOOD

When the Ancient Greeks brought civilization to the rest of the world – apart from America, which they didn't discover until 1492 and didn't really start colonizing until Kojak arrived in New York in the 1970s – one of the first gifts they bestowed was the concept of good food. The second was big helpings.

Until Alexander the Great defeated King Canute at Hastings, the Ancient Picts were living in trees, painting each other blue and getting by on fish fingers and oven chips. But when a Greek came home from a hard day's Socratic dialogue, he needed brain food. He needed *tahini, taramosalata, tzatziki, tabouleh, feta, halloumi, souvlaki, kebab, moussaka, dolmades, kleftiko, kalamari, stifado* and *baklava*, not baked beans on toast, and a decent cup of Greek coffee to wash it down, not a can of Fanta.

The main focus of a modern Greek's life is still food, but the fundamental mistake many beginners make is to serve it at a table that

only seats eight, or worse still, a kitchen breakfast bar. It just can't be done. The table must accommodate your wife, children, parents, in-laws, aunts, uncles, great-aunts and great-uncles, and all first cousins down to the twice removed. In other words, we're looking at something the size of the Cabinet table at 10 Downing Street, with extensions.

And the same is true of eating out. Whereas a Brit will say, 'Let's go to the seaside tomorrow and have a nice day out,' a Greek will say, 'I know this nice little restaurant near the seaside. Let's get a big table and have a good time, and maybe if there's some time left we can stroll along the seafront afterwards and get some ice cream and a couple of doughnuts.'

Put a Greek on his own in front of the telly with a meal on his lap and he's like a fish out of water. He also finds the silence unnerving. The most important ingredients of a Greek meal, you see, are the people you're eating it with, and the plates you can break afterwards.

HOW TO BE GREEK . . .
ABOUT HOSPITALITY

(a little bit)

If there are three little words that mean more to a Greek than any others, they have to be: 'Are you hungry?'

It's the single most important question you'll ever hear a Greek woman ask – and the most frequent.

When I was a child and I had my friends home to play, there was always food on the table, and plenty of it. I was reading Enid Blyton in those days, and was convinced my mum was the inspiration for the Famous Five's feasts of meatballs and rice with lashings and lashings of egg-lemon sauce.

'Demi,' she'd call lovingly up the stairs, 'ask Derek if he's hungry. And tell him to ring his mum and ask her if he can stay and eat.'

But any time I visited Derek's house, all I ever heard was a very different kind of yell from the kitchen: 'Oi, Del, your dinner's ready. Tell your mate to go home.'

You could be forgiven for thinking that the art of Greek hospitality is something you're born with, something you can never learn, no matter how hard you try. But just look at Nigella Lawson and Jamie Oliver. They were obviously at least a little bit Greek to start with, but you can't fault them now. My own English rose had a similar path to tread – but with just a little application and attention to detail, and a helping hand from her mother-in-law, she scaled Mount Olympus and came back down a fully fledged domestic goddess. True, she was propelled there by her undying love for the man she married, but there's no reason why you can't make the journey too.

When I was a teenager creeping upstairs some time after midnight (and here's a tip that any wife and mother would do well to note), my mum would fly out of her room at the first creak of the floorboards and ask if I was hungry.

Of course it was a question that could only have one answer, and a nice juicy steak would soon be sizzling under the grill.

Sometimes these days I'll say to my wife, 'Just popping out; only be a few minutes.' It's the least you can do when dinner's nearly ready.

HΦW TΦ BΣ GRΣΣK AT HΦMΣ

When I get back at two-thirty in the morning (owing to the unforeseen circumstance of Mick and me getting chatting and the boys coming round and the evening turning into a poker game), I can often be welcomed home by a deafening silence. Naturally enough, the first thing I do is wake my wife and ask what she cooked for me. I'd hate her to think her efforts hadn't been appreciated.

Poor woman, her Greek is good, but it isn't perfect, so 'Are you hungry?' can often sound a bit like 'I've chucked it in the bin.'

You can learn a lot from what I'm going to say next. As a beginner, your first step towards becoming a little bit Greek is to be realistic about what you can and can't achieve. Don't be too ambitious at the outset, but here's one golden tip that everyone can try at home: do unto others as you would have them do unto you. In other words, if you end up making yourself a sandwich as dawn approaches, always take a cigar and a glass of whisky upstairs with you. It saves your wife the trouble of fetching them for you when you've finished eating.

HOW TO BE
GREEK
AWAY

(a little bit)

HOW TO BE GREEK . . .
ON HOLIDAY

Greeks don't travel, as a rule – they emigrate. The only Greeks who ever spent a long time on the road were Jason and the Argonauts, and theirs was a long way from being a run-of-the-mill gap year.

Now, it's true I spent a year or two in Kos in my youth, but that was only because I had an auntie with a free room. And (a little bit) because the island was overrun with young female tourists. What's more, I had the edge over the other male tourists. Why me? It wasn't just about good looks, perfectly toned physique and raw sex appeal, as my best mate Mick never ceases to remind me. The edge I had over all the others was that I was a little bit Greek, and getting more so with every passing day.

Greeks Travel in Convoy

The great Greek emigrants had nothing on my granddad. When Columbus set sail from Athens on his epic voyage, all he ended up discovering was the New World. My granddad discovered Clacton. Well, strictly speaking, it was another Greek family from down the road in Balham who got there first, but from the way Papou went on about it, you could have sworn it was him.

I don't know about you, but when I was a kid I was backwards and forwards to Cyprus for my holidays. It was great, but we got dragged from house to house to make sure none of my aunties' noses were out of joint – and I had an awful lot of aunties. Some years all I saw was lunch tables.

Not that I was complaining, but I had heard rumours Cyprus had beaches.

The discovery of Clacton turned our lives upside down, and there's no reason why you can't share the magic.

A family from down the road had a chalet near the town. They asked my grandparents, who'd never heard of the place, if they'd like to use it for a week or so. It was for free, so of course they would – and obviously the whole family had to go. My mum drove my granddad, grandma, my brother and me in one car, and my uncles and their lot came in the rest of the convoy.

HOW TO BE GREEK AWAY

I'd never seen so many British people in one place. It was like a whole new world. There was so much open space that we could run around and get lost for the whole morning. We'd come back when Grandma was ready with lunch, then go off again until dinner. And this went on for six whole weeks.

Us Greek kids were popular. Yai Yai – my grandma – pushed fifty pence into our palms every day, so the Brits would come and ponce off us. Fifty pence went a long way on the arcade machines in those days. We lived like kings. Even Grandma got caught up in the whole adventure. A couple of evenings she'd take off her housecoat and say, 'Let's get fish and chips.'

We made more and more discoveries the longer we stayed. There was the Raven Club, which to me was like Vegas. We'd never seen cabaret. You don't see open talent contests in Greece or Cyprus. It was amazing to see a Brit get up and pretend to be Norman Wisdom. We sat there open-mouthed, my granny and me and my cousins, open-mouthed with a bottle of pop and bag of crisps she'd hidden in her handbag to keep costs down.

What to Wear in Clacton

Yai Yai would travel to Clacton in her normal clothes, but the minute she came through the door she'd slip on her housecoat. She wouldn't take it off until the end of the day, or unless we were going out. She would hang it by the front door, ready to put on the moment she got back in.

When we got back to Balham, you'd have thought she'd gone on a world cruise, the way she boasted to friends and neighbours about her exploits. I even saw her one day talking to the people down the road who'd lent us their chalet, explaining this and that to them like she'd lived there for years.

'No, they don't do *that*!' an auntie would gasp.

'Oh yes, that's the way they do things in Clacton,' Grandma would say, an old sweat at the exploration game.

Getting a Foot on the Property Ladder . . .

For my granny and my granddad it was the fulfilment of a dream, their own little piece of Cyprus within motoring distance of Balham.

HOW TO BE GREEK AWAY

It was near the sea, the food was excellent – and it came wrapped in a free newspaper.

Granddad knew which side his *pitta* was buttered. He bought a chalet as an investment. And then my uncle bought one. The Greeks are old hands at the colonization game.

The first thing they both did was go round with the incense to ward off the evil eye. That's something you never see Kirsty and Phil do. If you're ever on the show, take them a copy of this book. They could pick up a pointer or two.

. . . And Then the Other Foot, and Both Hands

Not content with one chalet, Granddad bought another, and another. As his property empire grew, more and more people wanted to borrow them and Granddad was happy to lend. Anything to store up a few favours.

Granddad's Empire

No sooner had my grandma set foot inside the door of her own chalet than a wipe-easy plastic cover appeared on the table and ornaments landed on every horizontal surface. Within days, the china donkeys and horses she'd brought down from Balham had been added to handsomely. The British would play bingo and save thousands of vouchers, but Grandma would win two or three and they'd burn a hole in her pocket. She'd always come back with something like a little horse with a trilby over his ears, pulling a cart, and if she'd had a big win the cart was full of toothpicks.

Granddad was in charge of exterior decor, and he pretty much took the Parthenon as his inspiration. None of the other lawns was mown, but Papou's was like a billiard table. The garden was absolutely pristine – if a little cluttered with statues of gods and goddesses around the Corinthian columns. Every trip they came down, the car was stuffed with more little touches. Clacton became a second home. Granddad built a little garden fence, painted it blue and white, and a BBQ appeared at the back.

HOW TO BE GREEK AWAY

Clacton was Granddad's little empire. It was only four chalets, but they brought him fifty pound a week each. He talked about Clacton the way Sir Ricky talks about Virgin. He would often say on a Friday night, 'Let's go to Clacton and check the business.'

'But, Granddad, what are you going to check? There are people in the chalets. You can't just walk in.'

'Yes, I know. But it's important to see and be seen.'

The Importance of Taking Something Back

No matter how short the stay, we always had to fill the car with manure for the return trip. We had to wander the fields with a bucket and spade, picking up cow shit to take back for Granddad's garden. When every square foot of his own was covered with brown, he'd give away the surplus.

'You can't find cow dung in Balham,' he used to say. 'People are thankful for it.'

It would stink the car out for an hour and a half, but it didn't matter. It was for Granddad. When we got home, we would unload the bags into the garden, and if there was any left over we'd phone Madame Elene from ten doors up. She would come down and collect her bag, and then it would be the Italians next door. There was a pecking order.

Grandma brought stuff back too. If someone came to our house she would pull out a stick of Clacton rock and present it like a scroll bestowing the freedom of the city. She might not have been to Clacton for three months, but people seemed happy to accept the gift. I suppose it was a lot easier to lug home than one of Granddad's manure bags.

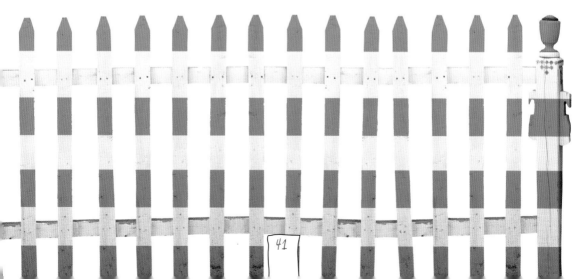

HOW TO BE A
GREEK GRANDDAD

HOW TO BE GREEK ... (a little bit of a)
LEGEND

Achilles. Adonis. Ajax. Apollo. Artemis. Athena. Atlas. And that's just the As. Greek mythology is stuffed full of legends you'll need to know about, and none more so than that mighty Greek Titan of the kitchen, the card table and the universe, known to me as Granddad.

Anything you did, my granddad would have done it bigger and better. The twelve labours of Hercules? Feats so difficult that they seemed impossible? I can almost hear Granddad's voice: 'I remember the time I had to clean out not one, but *two* Augean stables, and I still got to the market on time . . .'

The Twelve Labours of Papou

Granddad was a farmer. He was the best farmer. He grew the best vegetables. He would wake up at six in the morning, feed the animals, plough the fields, do this, do that. He'd gather all the fruit and veg and take it to the market. His journey to the market was the longest of any farmer in Cyprus, but he was always the first there and his fruit and veg were always the first to sell.

> *Faster, higher, stronger – Granddad embraced the Olympic motto with open arms*

He found water, he dug a well, and he got a pump that watered all the fields. His fields, as you might imagine, were the biggest fields, so you just accepted that his was the best pump, and that the water came from the deepest well.

Papou's achievements knew no bounds. When I said I was doing a bit of cabaret in a restaurant, the first thing he said was, 'I used to do a bit of theatre.'

'Oh, what theatre did you do, Papou?'

'I toured with a theatre group.'

I started a little football team for my son and his friends, and straight away it was, 'I was a football player.'

'When were you a football player?'

'I was famous in my village for being a football player. My village was the best team. We used to play all over Cyprus. Never once did we lose.'

The question I never asked, of course, was: 'From morning to night you were working the fields, taking the fruit and veg to market, then being Cyprus's answer to Laurence Olivier *and* Denis Law. Where did you find the time?'

Kitchen Confidential

It was at my uncle's restaurant where Papou's most famous story of his life as a Celebrity Masterchef came into being.

There had been this woman. She came to the restaurant almost every day to eat his moussaka, but one time she didn't come back for many, many months.

'Then one day, I was sitting in the kitchen and this woman comes in,' Papou said. '"Ah, Chef! Chef!" she cried. "How are you?" And I said, "Where have you been?" And do you know what she replied?' At this point he always puffed out his chest. 'She replied, "I have been away because I have been to *every* Greek restaurant *everywhere* in London, but I've come back to yours because you are the best!" She had tried all these moussakas everywhere, but – "Chef, yours is the best. And that's why I've come back and I'm here now to tell you." And I said to her, thank you, and go and sit down and I will bring you the moussaka.'

He would then add, with a slow nod of the head, 'And your uncle walked into the kitchen, and he said to me that she was sitting outside and she was eating the moussaka and she was very, very happy. And I said to him, "I knew she would come back. I told you she would come back."'

If I heard this story once, I must have heard it a thousand times. When he saw our eyes glaze over, he would round it off with the one about how he'd come out of the kitchen and people would applaud and say how great he'd been that day and how terrific the food was.

What could I do? He was Greek – exaggeration went with the territory.

If he was still alive today and saw this book, straight away it would have been, 'I was a little bit of a writer myself. . .'

(a little bit of a)

HOW TO BE GREEK . . .
PHILOSOPHER

Aristotle. Plato. Socrates. Papou. Their names line the Philosophers' Hall of Fame. Like all the great Greek thinkers, my granddad had something to say on most subjects, and it was nearly always worth listening to. Not necessarily ten times a day, but certainly at least once.

'YOU DON'T NEED TO SPEND MONEY.'

Apart from what goes on the mortgage, every penny a Greek granddad earns must go straight into the vault or under his mattress. The only thing he allows himself to spend big money on is a house.

When my new wife and I decided to get ourselves on the property ladder, Papou flipped over the mattress and handed us enough for the deposit. Yai Yai wasn't happy at first, but only because she'd been asleep at the time and landed awkwardly.

'THE UNDERGROUND IS THE BEST GREEK INVENTION SINCE SLICED BREAD. WHY YOU NEED A CAR?'

48

Nothing will ever shake a Greek granddad's belief that the tube was inspired by Orpheus in the Underworld. Or that Hovis isn't Greek.

'WORK HARD, PLAY CARDS HARD.'

Like the proper Greek granddad he was, Papou opened a café in Angel, Islington in the sixties that was effectively a gambling den. He paid a professional to sit down and play cards with whoever wanted a game. It was a big Greek thing back then. The Greeks would finish work on a Friday, collect their wages, and blow the lot by Monday morning.

To pay lip service to it being a café, they had a charcoal grill at the back and a little gas ring. They had a bed too. Some of the gamblers would be there right through the weekend and Granddad was on call to rustle up the coffee and kebabs at a moment's notice.

At Papou's café, food and drink was included with the game, and the house took a percentage of the card money. He treated the local police to a kebab so they'd leave him alone. It went on for years and years, until the dawn of Women's Lib and the advent of electronic payroll systems.

(a little bit of a)

HOW TO BE GREEK . . .
ERNST STAVROS BLOFELD

I have to admit I'm a bit concerned about where Ernst Stavros Blofeld fits into the family tree (about two generations back is the answer – but more of that in a minute), because I see myself as very much a Bond figure at the green baize.

Make no mistake: the typical Greek punter is not your betting shop type. Each ways, tricasts, exactas – they're girls' bets. Where's the glory in backing horses and dogs to come second or third? If you're serious about being at least a little bit Greek, you need to man up. It's all or nothing for you. And that means a serious game of poker, winner takes all.

Big Deal

No Greek card game is complete without the Look. Cigar smoke curling towards the ceiling. The clink of ice in whisky glasses. A beautiful woman coming and going with stuffed olives and grilled *halloumi* on a stick.

You must clench your whisky glass in your fist, with your little finger raised ever so slightly, slam it down on the table from time to time, and slap anyone within reach manfully on the shoulder. The rule of thumb here is that if your behaviour might start a brawl in any other surroundings, you've got it more or less right.

Show Them Who's Boss

A hairy chest can't be taught – but you can learn how to *think* a little bit Greek. You must show the other guys round the table who wears the trousers in your house. As long as you've got your wife's permission.

Picture a semi-circle of tables laden with food. Wine and whisky flow. Music and dancing won't be far behind. The evening will get loud and raucous, but it won't get out of hand. Everyone wants to carry on until dawn. They don't want to collapse, bladdered, outside the Dog & Donkey as soon as Happy Hour's over.

I don't drink more than a little bit, but I love seeing a bottle of Black Label on the table. My granddad never understood my abstinence. He'd say to me, 'Have a little more whisky.'

'But, Papou, I don't drink much.'

'It's good that you don't drink much. Just have a little bit more.'

It was the same with smoking. He loved his pipe. And of course, he knew more about tobacco blends than Peter Stuyvesant and Philip Morris put together – which was pretty much what he did. In his later years he took to cutting up basil leaves and mixing them with his ready rubbed. The doctor and the priest both told him to pack it in.

'But I'm eighty-five,' he'd say to them. 'What's the point? OK, Doc – see you and raise you fifty.'

And that's sort of where we come back to the villain with the cat in his lap. Granddad used to take me to all the Bond movies, and it goes without saying that, fantastic as they were, he could always see room for improvement.

Anyway, it was he who decided that a far better name for the man with the cat was Ernst Stavros Blofeld.

And come to think of it, the cat wasn't quite right either. . .

HOW TO BE A

GREEK
DAD

HOW TO BE A GREEK DAD

(a little bit)

HOW TO BE GREEK . . .
ABOUT YOUR CHILDREN

A Greek dad's biggest fear is that his teenage daughter will run into a Greek boy wearing the same expression that he used to at that age. As Papou used to say: 'Raise a Greek daughter? It would be easier to raise the _Titanic_.'

You can quite happily give your boy a wink and a nudge as he goes out, and say, 'Go on, my son, make jiggy-jiggy while the sun shines.' But your daughter? Ideally, you lock her up and throw away the key until her thirtieth birthday.

It's not an entirely level playing field, but that's what being a little bit Greek is all about. Why go to all the trouble of inventing the word hypocrisy if you don't actually use it on a regular basis? Back in Greece, this leads to what Plato called scarcity of resources. If everyone's locking away their daughters, who is there for the sons to have jiggy-jiggy with? Step forward the generous Swedes, Germans, Irish and British . . .

'Things My Dad Would Never Say'

That said, I'm not sure my own daughter takes me too seriously in these matters. She made me a Father's Day card this year headed *Things My Dad Would Never Say*. It was a long list. It included:

'Why don't you invite a few boys around?'

'When you do, would you mind keeping your bedroom door closed because the music's too loud?'

'I think we should both get some new tattoos.'

And:

'Here's twenty quid, go out and get bladdered.'

GOLDEN RULES
FOR RAISING A GREEK DAUGHTER

- Restrict her TV viewing to Little House on the Prairie or anything starring Jacques Cousteau.

- You can brag to your friends about how beautiful and smart she is, but tell them to make sure their sons stay away.

- At the earliest opportunity, give her a brace, a bad haircut, lots of chocolate and hope for the best.

HOW TO BE . . .
GREEK DAD

(a little bit of a)

My granddad taught me everything he thought I needed to know. My best mate Mick taught me most of the things Papou didn't think I needed to know. And just being Greek taught me the rest.

It is now my responsibility to pass on this wealth of folklore, myth and legend to my own children. My daughter Elle won't be allowed out alone until her thirtieth birthday, so until then the huge responsibility of being a Greek at large falls on my son Lagi's shoulders.

> *Not every successful man is a good father, but every good father is a successful man*

It's not always a straightforward process. Some of Papou's Lessons in Life did puzzle me when I was young. His assertion, for example, that 'If it has tyres or teats it's going to give you problems' had me scratching my head until I was at least eight.

> **One day, my son, all this will be yours**

Raising a daughter mostly entails a brief guided tour of the kitchen, shredding any mail that smells of Clearasil and telling her you have to be over twenty-five to join Facebook. Beyond that, your duties as a father are limited to thirty years of escorting her to and from school, catering college, church and Greek socials.

But a son – a son you have to teach everything in this book, and (a little bit) more besides.

Some people think that being (a little bit) Greek is child's play. They see a few Greek tragedies (twice nightly if they'd been in my restaurant kitchen) and think: love, jealousy, betrayal, remorse, yeah, the Greeks have got the big emotions sorted. Needless to say, there's a lot more to it than that, both on and off the football pitch.

Football

Football may well be the most important thing that a father can teach his son – which is why the Greeks invented football. The only problem is that

despite Greece's famous World Cup victory I knew next to nothing about football when I arrived in England. I could play a little bit but I didn't know any players' names or anything.

When my son Lagi was eight, my English rose decided it was time to take him to a football academy thing. She does nothing by halves, my wife – she signed us up to sponsor the team for £500 as well. I was terrified of betraying my ignorance, and couldn't decide whether to adopt the Al Fayed swagger or sit quietly on the bench.

I sat quietly on the bench.

This went on every Wednesday night for three or four weeks, until the season started. I didn't shout anything from the sidelines, I just sat there quietly. After about four or five games, I couldn't help noticing that a number of the kids never played, and Lagi was one of them. He was always a substitute.

It started to get on my nerves. These kids deserved a fair crack of the whip. Eventually I told the manager, 'Look, I didn't want to say anything, but I think that at eight years old everyone deserves a shot. This isn't the European Championships!'

'I've been doing this for ten years,' he said, 'and I know that if you don't play the good players and win, people will leave.'

We went round and round in circles. In the end I decided to start my own team. I went off and bought all the kit. I had this vision: I'd get all the really bad kids together, perform the kind of miracle that you only ever see in Little League Baseball movies, win the league against all the odds, the kids would carry me around the stadium, shoulder-high . . .

We were shit. We had the worst scores. We had the worst record, seven fixtures without a goal. And I spent every one of them running up and down the sidelines, still not knowing a thing about the game, shouting encouragement and disputing decisions. I didn't have a clue about the offside rule, but that didn't hold me back.

We ended up second from the bottom, but I played every kid. Everyone got a go. I gave everyone a little bit of silver for their mantelpiece. I never did get carried anywhere shoulder-high, but our trophy days were the best trophy days in the world.

HOW TO BE A GREEK DAD

You Can Whistle for It

I'm such a paranoid father that as soon as Lagi could walk I made a deal with him: whenever I whistled, he had to come running. I've got quite a loud whistle, and I was scared of losing him. It still works now.

We were at Butlin's yesterday and Lagi hired a bike with his mate. I didn't know where he was for about five minutes. His mate's mum was cool as a cucumber, but I got in a real state. So I whistled and up popped this head like a meerkat. It's our party piece.

Mick thinks it's bad, like I'm whistling for a dog, but it's not as if I'm getting him to round up sheep or anything. I tried that, but it never worked. We still have to go to the butcher for our *kleftiko*.

Talking . . . and Not Forgetting to Listen

I can bargain with Lagi. I can always strike a deal with him. We sit down and discuss everything, from what we're going to have for dinner to the mysteries of the universe. We'll go through the good points and the bad points, what's right and what's wrong. He'll ask a thousand questions.

I'll tell him the answers the way I see them. The Greeks love talking; it's in our genes – but it can be learned.

My daughter Elle can talk the hind leg off a ceramic donkey, but listening isn't high on her list of priorities. She's a great kid, but basically, she doesn't give a monkey's. After an hour or two of spirited debate with her, I'll sometimes have to bring out the big guns. Mick can always be relied upon to tell her what's what.

Every One a Winner

We all went to a holiday park together when the kids were younger. They went in for a dancing competition. There were prizes and everything: little medals that you hang round your neck.

Mick slipped off for a couple of minutes as the awards ceremony drew to a close. The MC suddenly popped back onto the stage to make another announcement. 'And ladies and gentlemen . . . a prize we forgot to give out earlier . . . to Mr Lagi Demetriou!'

Mick gave me a big Greek grin. He'd bunged the geezer a tenner. They got such shit wages, the guy had probably never seen one before. Even now, I don't have the heart to tell Lagi how he got his first dance prize. He'd never stop wondering if Mick had had a quiet word with Simon Cowell.

Heroes, Not Zeroes

Every dad wants to be a hero to his son. And not just round the BBQ.

We were on the beach in Cyprus a while back, all of us together. I can never sit still. Lagi usually can't either. My English rose and our Elle stretch out on the sunbeds, but me and Lags are always in the water.

I glanced out to sea and noticed that someone had tipped over one of those little sailboat things they hire out. I waited, and looked, and it still hadn't popped back up. So I collared the guy at the kiosk. 'There's a boat out there,' I said. 'They've tipped it over and it's not getting back up.'

He goes, 'I'll go and take a look.'

I go, 'I'll come with you.'

He gave his throttle some welly and we pulled alongside the bloke who'd capsized.

'Thanks very much,' he said.

'No problems,' I replied modestly.

I made myself useful as we pulled the sailboat in. I stood at the bow and held my arms out, like Leonardo di Caprio in *Titanic*.

There was no hero's welcome back at the beach. I walked to where the girls were still flat out on their sunbeds and said, 'You needn't have worried. I just had to go out and save some guy.' No one was listening.

I went, 'Yeah, he was in a bit of trouble, but we got the speedboat out.' I'm talking away and no one's paying the slightest attention.

Eventually Lagi turned up. 'What are you talking about, Dad?'

I shrugged matter-of-factly. 'I just saved someone.'

Lagi's eyebrows disappeared beneath his fringe. 'Yeah, yeah, yeah.'

Anyway, about twenty minutes later this guy came up with a little baby in his arms, and he stood there and everyone turned round, and he said, 'I just want to thank you, mate. You saved this little girl's dad.'

I couldn't have written it any better if I'd tried.

'I could have drowned out there,' he said. You should have seen their faces. That was me, the hero dad. I milked it for the whole of the rest of the holiday. Well, I'm still going strong today, to be honest.

GROWING UP GREEK

(a little bit)

HOW TO BE GREEK . . .
ON MOTHER'S DAY

One of the few businesses you'll never see under Greek ownership is an old people's home. You've got to love, respect, honour and obey your parents, and look after them till the end. Especially your mum. She's special: look who she gave birth to.

- ❻ When the neighbour's son turns up on Mother's Day with a big bunch of daffodils and she asks your mum, 'Did your son bring you flowers?' your mum must be able to answer, 'But my son brings me flowers every day.'

- ❻ You must expect to go to your parents' for lunch every Sunday until your mum's ninety-five and the rheumatism finally gets too much for her to cook for twenty-six and clear the plates away single-handed. That's when she moves in with you, can finally put her feet up, and comment on how slow your wife is round the house.

HOW TO BE GREEK ... *(a little bit)*
BEHIND THE WHEEL

Like many of the lessons in this book, what follows is a bit of a cautionary tale. I had something of a brush with the law when I was a kid, as you'll discover.

There was this public car park we used as a shortcut to school. One day on the way through we found some keys on top of one of the cars. I decided it would be cool if we opened the door, so I took them off the roof and did just that. We sat in it, giggled, got out again and went on our way.

Next day, the Vauxhall was still there – and so were the keys. How could a red-blooded thirteen-year-old resist? I popped the key in the ignition to see what happened, and what happened was that the engine started up. I'd watched my hero Theo Kojak enough times to know what to do next. I didn't have a lollipop, so instead I put the car in gear and drove it round the car park. In no time I was tearing around, chasing imaginary bad guys through the Bronx. *Who loves ya, baby?*

We went to school, and an hour later a policeman came into my classroom. 'Can we see Mr Demetriou?'

They called out my mates' names too, escorted us all from the building and took us to the police station. I was in an interview room when I heard the screech of tyres, followed a minute or two later by raised voices. I guessed there was some big bust going on.

The voices got louder, and my mum burst into the room.

'Right, that's it – you wait till your granddad hears about this.'

Plea Bargaining

The police let me off with a warning. They could see that whatever was coming my way from my mother was worse than anything they could inflict. And besides, her car was blocking the station entrance.

My mum put a deal to me. She'd found out that the estate agents at the top of the road had alerted the cops. 'You're going in there first thing to thank them for telling the police.'

'But, Mum . . .'

'If you don't, I'll tell your granddad.'

Job done. Papou was in Cyprus, but he'd be back any day now.

I didn't take the shortcut next morning. I went the long way round, via the estate agents. Bright red with embarrassment, I went in. 'Is Mr Jones here?' I said. 'I just want to thank you for calling the police on me.'

'You what?'

I went, 'Thank you very much,' and walked out.

My granddad had hardly landed at Luton before my mum had grassed me up. I'd kept my end of the deal, but she told him regardless. There was some kind of family oneupmanship going on – she had to tell him before one of my aunties did.

I was upstairs at my granddad's house, waiting. I got the call to come down. My granddad had never hit me, never laid a finger on me. (The Greek approach to child development and discipline is very much calorie-based.) But there's a first time for everything, and I was thinking, 'This is it, trouble with the police. He's going to kill me.'

I told him the whole story, and when I'd finished, he looked at me for a long time and finally said, 'I'm really disappointed. You're supposed to be Greek. A Jaguar, I could understand. . .'

(a little bit)

HOW TO BE GREEK ...
ON YOUR SAINT'S DAY

St Wayne, St Darren, St Kylie, St Chantelle – I'm sorry, but even for us Greeks, some things are impossible. The church hasn't canonized any of these guys yet, so you can't be baptized with their names.

For the rest of us, though, our saint's day is very important. On it, all our friends and family must phone us, and if they see us, buy us cakes.

Bad luck, Piers and Amanda – it looks like Simon gets all the doughnuts.

HOW TO BE GREEK . . .
DETECTIVE

The Greeks might set great store by family, big weddings, looking after your mates and cracking boys over the head with dustbin lids if they mess with your sister, but that doesn't make my godfather Don Corleone.

Can you think of a single Greek (apart from Del Trotter) who's ever been on the wrong side of the law? The Trojan Horse was a bit of a scam, but that was a long time ago and all in a good cause. You don't get emails every five minutes from the chief most important accountant of the Bank of North Kos wishing you God's blessings and presenting to you an urgent and confidential request for your account details so he can send you your 27 billion drachma lottery win.

No, the Greeks just don't do crime. Though if they did, of course, they'd probably be the most successful criminals in the world.

Instead, we've provided most of the great seekers after justice and truth over the years:

Kojak – obviously.

Cracker – ask yourself, could anyone who's obviously enjoyed so many hot dinners be anything but Greek? (Calories are a great Greek invention, of course, and big Fitz knew you need to put away as many as possible, just in case of emergencies.)

The Saint – with a halo like that, what else could he be?

Jack Frost – or come to think of it, any detective played by David Jason and the Argonauts.

And, finally, **Columbo** – OK, the rumpled raincoat was a bit off-message, but in all other respects the man with the cigar at the murder scene was truly one of us. When he makes to leave, only to turn back with all eyes upon him as he utters the immortal, dramatic line, 'Just one more thing . . .' what you have there, ladies and gentlemen, is pure, unadulterated, 100 per cent quintessential Greek.

(a little bit)

HOW TO BE GREEK . . .
IN A QUEUE

If you're a patient sort of soul, you might have a bit of an uphill struggle becoming as Greek as you'd like to be. Just give impatience a go, and if at first you don't succeed, be Greek and try something else.

To a Greek, you see, delayed gratification is waiting ten seconds for a chip to cool. But we're the first to understand that being incapable of waiting for anything, from money to sex, doesn't come naturally to everyone, especially a queue-loving nation like the British. We're happy to make allowances.

If you ever see a Greek standing in a queue, watch and learn. He's only there while he's trying to work out a way of leapfrogging to the front.

That's why Samsung is one of Greece's top companies. Their slogan is: 'Impatience is a virtue.' You can't get more Greek than that.

HOW TO BE GREEK . . .
ON AND OFF THE PITCH

The Greeks might have invented the Olympics, but the only sports you should watch or take part in these days are the ones you can have really loud opinions about.

The best we managed in Beijing was a silver for rowing. No matter; we cheered the news long into the night. It was only when we discovered that this rowing just involved sitting around in a very thin boat and never arguing about the route or grabbing a netful of *kalamari* that we turned our attention elsewhere.

When I was a young man, tennis was quite high on the list. These days it's only a little bit Greek when Andy Murray takes to the court and looks like he's about to chin the umpire; you can hardly describe a polite, quietly spoken Swiss geezer as the ideal ambassador for the game. But back then the cat-gut really used to go with a twang. John McEnroe and Jimmy Connors knew the meaning of the word 'racket', and no mistake. These days, we can be proud of Greek wonderboy Rafa Nadal's manly grunts – though I do worry about the unpicking of the wedgie while he's waiting to receive serve.

Rugby may look like Greek dancing with a more complicated set of rules, but football remains the most beautiful of all Greek games. It goes without saying that any player or manager called George must be Greek, especially if he has black hair and is extremely good-looking. No way can you tell me the legendary George Best wasn't from Famagusta.

Greece, of course, won the World Cup in 2004. I didn't watch the final against Portugal myself, but as soon as I found out we were world champions I jumped in the car and drove up and down Cockfosters Road, waving a Greek flag and hooting my horn. The lesson you can take away from this is clear. If you truly want to be a little bit Greek, then you mustn't be afraid of either milking a victory or jumping on a bandwagon. The day these two pursuits are finally acknowledged as Olympic sports, we'll have more gold medals on the mantelpiece than ceramic donkeys.

HOW GREEK IS YOUR LOVE?

(a little bit)

HOW TO BE GREEK . . .
IN THE DISCO

When I was twelve or so, you'd never have got me and my cousins into a pub. We wanted to talk to women, and about a whole lot more than the England team's chances against Brazil. Discos were our hunting ground, and not just because 'discos' is a Greek word.

We took our lead from top Greek role model John Travolta, and Maximus in Leicester Square was *the* venue for a bit of *Saturday Night Fever*. Even the name was right. You half expected to see Kirk Douglas under the glitter ball, showing off some moves with his short sword.

A few years later, when almost everybody else in my class was still fantasizing about getting served a pint, the Greeks set the bar a bit higher. It was all about how many girls you could chat up and how many telephone numbers you could write down. Sometimes, out of pity, we took our British friends along. I looked upon these sessions very much as tutorials in How To Be (a little bit) Greek:

- **Get inside her personal space** You don't have to be as Greek as George Clooney to work out that if a girl lets you close enough to chat her up, she isn't pigeon-holing you alongside Fungus the Bogeyman. She's prepared to let this cheeky Greeky chappy set out his stall; she wants to know Today's Special Offer.

- **Show her what you've got** What I always offered was to take them out for a meal – and by that I mean a proper sit-down at my uncle's restaurant in Cheam (where I worked), not a saveloy and a bag of chips on the Thames Embankment.

- **Can't get enough** Whether it's money or women, a Greek wants more. I got my first car when I was seventeen and that was it, I'd hit the jackpot. Because I had a job, I always had a nice big wad in my pocket to show the girls I was pleased to see them, and now I could drive them to some of the nicest places in town. It certainly made a nice change from the alleyway behind Morrison's.

(a little bit)

HOW TO BE GREEK . . . AT A WEDDING

One of the quickest ways to be a little bit Greek is to marry one. And it doesn't matter where you come from. My grandparents didn't bat an eyelid when I said I was marrying a foreigner. All these years, I'd been thinking they wanted me to marry a nice Greek girl – but all they really wanted was for me to marry. The family unit is what counts – and as this book shows, there's always time, with the right kind of tuition, to become a little bit Greek later. When your child comes of age, the only questions a grandparent will be asking are who and when?

Greek In-laws

Greek mother-in-laws can be a nightmare, which was one of the reasons I chose an English rose as my wife. The other, of course, was that I love her. (Now stop looking over my shoulder, will you, and go and make me a sandwich.)

It's difficult for Greek in-laws. They can't stop themselves getting involved. Whilst the Brits let a couple get on with it, the Greeks are always interfering. But their intentions are good. As long as the couple is happy, they're happy – oh yeah, as long as they're pumping out babies.

When my wife came into our family, it was: 'Well, now you're Greek.' She'd married a Greek, she must be Greek. Often they'd talk to her in Greek.

'But, Papou, she doesn't understand a word.'

'She'll pick it up.'

And do you know what? She did.

One of the quickest ways to be a little bit Greek is to marry one

How to Have a Big Fat Greek Wedding

STEP ONE: THE MONEY

The going rate for a wedding reception is £30 per head, and I don't mean for the catering. I mean the cash you have to pin on the bride. Add £50 a head to be paid by each of the fifty best men and fifty best women, and a few thou from the parents and grandparents, and you can see how it adds up. It's all clear profit for the newly married couple, too, because the parents will have footed the bill.

STEP TWO: THE GUEST LIST

Weddings are huge for Greeks. Everything about them is on a massive scale. The guest list. The venue. The number of best men. The mountain of Coke cans for the kids to turn into mortar bombs. Invite fewer than 500 people to a Greek wedding and they'll call you Stavros No-Mates. I had 501 at mine, just to be on the safe side.

STEP THREE: THE VENUE

Greek weddings are held on Sundays, which is good news for British hotels. They can have a nice refined British wedding on the Saturday, and a big fat Greek one twenty-four hours later.

STEP FOUR: THE CEREMONY

The groom has to get dressed at his house, the bride at hers. There's a priest at each address to ward off the evil eye and any pre-marital hanky-panky.

When they finally get together, the parents and the grandparents pass a red ribbon round the betrothed three times.

If the man steps on the woman's foot when they're taking their vows, it means he's going to be the boss. That doesn't happen so much these days. And I can tell you that if you're marrying an English rose, you don't stand a chance.

The priest says everything three times during the ceremony – not because he's got Alzheimer's, but in honour of the Holy Trinity. Then he takes the couple round the altar three times. The Best Man stands behind the groom, and the other forty-nine best men slap him on the back because he's meant to be there to protect the groom. It seems to be a point of honour to try and dislodge a shoulder blade.

STEP FIVE: THE MAIN EVENT

The most important part of the ceremony, of course, is the food and drink afterwards.

The tables groan with the stuff. I know that for a fact – I sat under hundreds of them as an eight-year-old. Girls wear their best dresses to weddings, and opportunities like that can't be passed up.

The table-tops are covered with bottles of wine, whisky and brandy, and hundreds of cans of beer and American champagne – or Coca-Cola as it's sometimes called. As soon as our parents tell the kids they can get down from the table, they grab as many of them as they can and make a bee-line for the car park.

STEP SIX: THE ENTERTAINMENT

You start by establishing the pecking order. The oldest has first throw. You lob the can as high into the air as possible. It splits when it hits the ground and spins like a foaming Catherine wheel. It's the most fun you can have as an eight-year-old unless you're still under a table.

An hour or fifty Coke cans later, the girls go one way, the boys the other. The under-twelve boys go in search of more Coke cans, and the over-twelves discuss the view from under the table.

STEP SEVEN: DID I MENTION THE MONEY?

The big moment has arrived. The bride stands and all 501 guests take a pin from a best woman's cushion and fasten crisp ten and twenty pound notes to her dress. It's a joy to behold – as much as twenty grand, and all in cash.

The money dance is all about giving the young couple a good start. None of this our-list-is-at-Peter-Jones nonsense. A Greek couple's wedding list is at NatWest.

No wonder Greek brides don't stint on the lace. When Diana married Charles, hers ran the length of St Paul's and halfway down Cheapside. I couldn't help wondering if her father-in-law had had a hand in it.

STEP EIGHT: THE HAPPY COUPLE DEPART

Weddings are a big deal as a kid. It's a chance to make new friends, and to start compiling the guest list for your own wedding.

As a grown-up, they're an even bigger deal.

Our parents forked out £16,000 for our wedding, and my wife came away with £13,000 pinned to her dress. Poor girl, she could hardly stagger to the car, what with all the suitcases she was carrying as well.

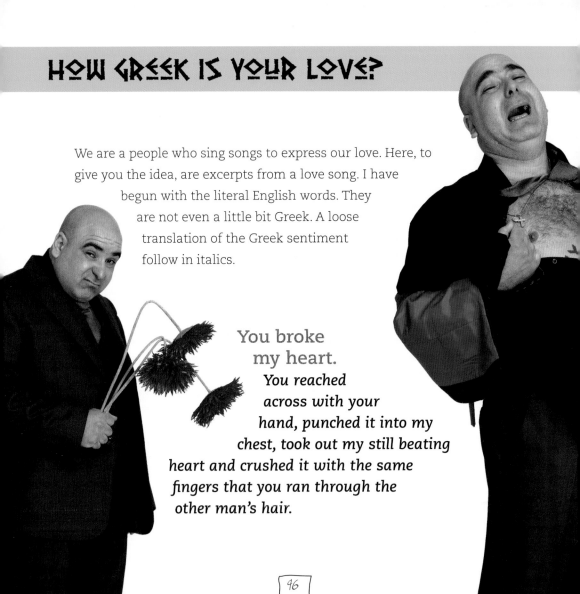

HOW GREEK IS YOUR LOVE?

We are a people who sing songs to express our love. Here, to give you the idea, are excerpts from a love song. I have begun with the literal English words. They are not even a little bit Greek. A loose translation of the Greek sentiment follow in italics.

You broke my heart.
You reached across with your hand, punched it into my chest, took out my still beating heart and crushed it with the same fingers that you ran through the other man's hair.

46

I drank to forget you.

I drank . . . I smoked . . . I danced all night to forget the pain that you inflicted on me. You ruined my life!

You're beautiful.

I can see the sunlight in your emerald eyes and the fire from your lips will consume me after I have been lost in your soul.

I would like to see you again.

If I don't see you again I will die a thousand deaths and feel the pain of a sword piercing my lonely heart like a skewer through pig's flesh.

GREEK

IN

MIND
BODY
SPIRIT

(a little bit)

HOW TO BE GREEK . . .
IN MIDDLE AGE

One of the greatest things about being a Greek male is that the older you get, the more attractive you become. It's no accident that the Ancient Greeks still live in legend. No wonder it's every young boy's dream, almost from birth, to look like Anthony Quinn in *Zorba the Greek* as soon as he can. Early-onset sideburns mean that an eight-year-old can chat up a girl in Year 6, and by the time he's fifteen and is being let into West End discos because he looks twenty-one, the world's his *kalamari*.

If you're a Brit, you could be forgiven for asking at this point, 'Why would anyone want to look older? Youthful and handsome clinches the deal every time.' To which I'd answer, 'Tell that to Demis Roussos.'

There's many a fine tune played on an old bouzouki

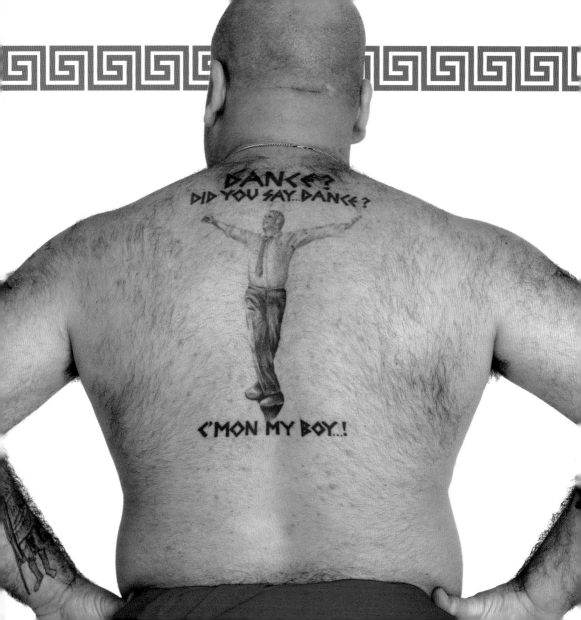

Or to the former president of Greece who fell for a young air hostess in the eighties – which was also pretty much his age at the time.

Then of course there was the handsome Silvio Berlusconi, though he's no longer Greek these days. We embraced him as one of our own until he went down the hair-weave *autostrada*.

But I don't want you thinking that being old and Greek is only about not borrowing someone else's rug. Captain Kirk didn't baldly go where so many Greeks have gone before, but he's as Greek today as he ever was. He went the syrup route too, but remained very manly on the flight deck of the *Enterprise* – which is after all a Greek concept. And while we're on the subject of rugs, look at Bruce Forsyth. He's 100 per cent Greek. The women still love him, and he can still tap-dance like there's no tomorrow.

Dean Martin drank like a Greek, and so did Inspector Morse. Jag keys in one hand, a glass of the good stuff in the other – you can't get much more Greek than that. George Clooney is one of us too. He went grey and the women didn't bat an eyelid.

Some people think the enduring appeal of the ageing Greek is just about owning a fleet of BBQs. That couldn't be further from the truth.

It's sometimes about owning ships as well. Mao Tse Tung was a wise old bird (although he never became more than a little bit Greek). When he was asked how the world might have changed if President Khrushchev had been assassinated instead of President Kennedy, he didn't hesitate for more than a moment before saying that he doubted very much that Ari Onassis would have married Mrs Khrushchev.

Wrinkles Rule

The Brits worship the young. Harry Potter, coke-snorting catwalk models, Ferrari-trashing footballers – it doesn't seem to matter. But what do they know about the secrets of the universe? The Greeks look up to anyone who's a bit older, more distinguished, more philosophical.

Greek women will look at an older man and say, 'I bet he's been round the block a few times and has a tale or two to tell.' And where they lead, others follow. The girls love a bit of rough and rugged. More wrinkles, not fewer – that's the name of the game. You'll never see a jar of Nivea for Men on the front table in a Greek beauty parlour. As Aristotle so rightly said: 'It's because I'm worth it.'

(a little bit)

HOW TO BE GREEK . . .
IN OLD AGE

There are no nursing homes in Greece. The only place we put old people is at the head of the table. And gyms don't get a look in, even though we invented them.

In Cyprus they built these lovely two-mile promenades along the seafront. At the end of the night, the older (and thus more desirable) Greek men get together and start strolling. They're lovely promenades, and the food stalls lining the way enhance the view. But the old boys aren't just after the ice cream and doughnuts – that's just the icing on the cake. They're there because they have a duty to perform. They might be stopped at any moment and asked the Meaning of Life. It never happens, but they're ready with the answers if it does.

HOW TO BE GREEK . . .
IN THE LABOUR WARD

(a little bit)

Childbirth can be a very trying time for a Greek. Traditionally, it used to entail long hours of pacing up and down a hospital corridor with a cigar in one hand and a whisky in the other, but these days they make you go outside.

I can only imagine it's because if your wife is halfway through labour and she catches a whiff of Black Label and a King Edward, she's going to feel compelled to jump off the bed and come and make sure you've got enough ice. By the time she's run back and forth with that and the ashtray she forgot first time round, the baby stands a good chance of being born in the car park.

If this happens, whatever you do, don't panic. Seize the chance to jump in the Jag and head home sharpish to fire up the BBQ before the boys arrive.

(a little bit)

HOW TO BE GREEK . . .
FOR EVER

The Greeks have had a love affair with doctors and tablets since the day Hippocrates prescribed the first aspirin.

When my family came over here, there was a famous doctor called Zacharias. He was from our village, and he was almost as revered as the butcher.

Anything wrong with us, it was off to Zacharias. You'd go in, your grandparents would have a twenty-minute chat with him and they'd eventually get on to the ailment.

At this point he would reach for his prescription pad. It didn't matter what kind of tablet was involved, he would add a few extra because it was my grandparents and they came from the same village. This happened everywhere there were Greeks, so sometimes we didn't even bother going to the doctor. We'd just do our own diagnosis. Pull open any drawer at random and you'd find enough medicine to treat a whole county.

'I've saved these from last time. Take them.'

'But, Grandma, it's not prescribed for me.'

'Zacharias gave it to me for the same thing – it must be all right.'

When Co-codamol arrived on the scene, it was like my grandparents had hit the jackpot: an extra-strength painkiller that sounded a little bit Greek. They hoarded boxes and boxes of the stuff all over the house. The donkey on the mantelpiece even had a pack in one of his side baskets – and a few more under his trilby, for all I knew.

One Size Cures All

We have a drink called Zivania. It's like ouzo, only 45 per cent proof. It's basically surgical spirit, and Greeks swear by it. Zivania's the remedy for everything. If it hurts, rub some Zivania on it. If that doesn't work, tilt your head back and swallow. If I started sniffing, my grandparents would splash it on all over and rub me up and down. For the next three days I'd be terrified of going near a naked flame.

A cold was never just a cold, of course. With a Greek child, there's no such thing as a minor ailment. You have to be *really* looked after, and

that means soup. Cauldrons of the stuff. From there you move on to *glikaniso* – herbal tea – and if that doesn't shift it, then it's time for Zivania.

Château Cockfosters

Anthropologists down Cockfosters way have been baffled for years as to why a Greek will always sniff a bottle of water before drinking from it, but at last I can tell you why.

We had an Italian next-door neighbour who'd once shown Granddad how to make wine, so no prizes for guessing who announced, on the strength of one dodgy batch of grapefruit champagne, that he was probably the best wine-maker on the entire planet. It was terrible. It was the only wine I'd ever seen with more sediment than liquid.

Later on, when he came to live with my mum and was banned from using the bath as a brewery, he turned his hand to cocktails. He'd pour water onto herbal leaves and let them steep for a few days, then add this secret ingredient to whisky, brandy, whatever was going. It tasted disgusting, which made him think it must be good for you.

It wasn't long before Papou branched out into the home-brewed Zivania business. Any bottle you emptied, you knew not to throw away – even a plastic water bottle. You put it to one side of the sink and Papou would take it from there.

We gave it away as fast as he could make it, and before long, Papou's Zivania was the toast of Cockfosters – well, according to its manufacturer. He never bothered to change the labels though, and a lot of thirsty people got a shock. And that's why, to this day, whenever a Greek is given a bottle of water he'll give it a precautionary sniff.

(a little bit)

HOW TO BE GREEK . . .
IN RELIGIOUS MATTERS

The church is really important to a lot of Greeks, mainly the elderly with at least half an eye on the future. My grandmother used to go to church every Sunday, and would always come back spitting teeth about the sermon.

'The priest was terrible today, even worse than last week. I can't believe he said all these things.'

'So, Grandma, why do you keep going back?'

'Because I want go to heaven.'

I could never understand her. Why would anyone need heaven when they already had Cockfosters?

When we first moved to this little piece of north London paradise, the priest ran a stamp club in his cottage next to the church. My mother sent me over and I became an avid collector. I collected stamps for years and years, some of them really valuable. The priest took a huge interest in my

album, and spent many an hour with
his magnifying glass, turning the pages
or reading what he called 'a specialist
magazine' that he'd never let me see. From
time to time he'd send me off on long errands, and it was
only much later that I found out why.

When I got married, I decided to insure my stamp collection. It was
my most valuable possession by far. Or so I thought.

I went to an upmarket dealer in Mayfair and proudly presented my
album. He looked through it, with an expression I interpreted as quietly
impressed.

I gave him a nod and said, 'So how many thou should I cover it for?'

'Well to be honest, sir,' he said, 'I'd offer you three pounds for the
album – but you'd be better off keeping the stamps. Some of them can
still be used.'

I still have that album, and I have my suspicions. It was that dodgy
priest – he wasn't just admiring my Penny Blacks when he sent me to
the shops, he was swapping them with fakes.

(a little bit)

HOW TO BE GREEK ...
ABOUT SUPERSTITIONS

Greeks are so superstitious we'll knock on wood and spit three times as soon as we hear the word. Personally I've never been bothered with any of that mumbo-jumbo. The charms I wear round my neck take care of that sort of stuff.

It starts at birth. Your nappy will be fastened with a gold safety pin that carries the Big Three – the evil eye, a St Christopher and a crucifix. For the next few months you'll be watching and listening anxiously from your pram in case some idiot says you're cute – in which case your nan's salivary glands will go into overdrive.

Throughout your childhood, whenever someone compliments you, your grandmother or mother will fly to your defence. 'Nice? *Nice?* What do you mean by *nice?*' The problem is that a compliment is never taken at face value. We know there's something else behind it. When someone says to you, 'I like that shirt,' you know full well that what he really means is, 'I wish I had that shirt.' And when jealousy is on the premises, all sorts of bad things will start to happen – unless you strike back.

The first thing to do is hurl a piece of prime Greek invective at whoever's dared compliment you, such as: 'Stick your evil eye back up where the sun don't shine.' Then you touch your own evil eye. Carrying an evil eye works the same way as homeopathy (another Greek invention, naturally). You wear the evil eye to keep away the evil eye. It makes perfect sense. Every Greek house has one over the door to protect the occupants against those who covet the ornaments on their mantelpiece.

Warding Off the Evil Eye

There are those who are said to know how to remove the eye from someone who is affected. The church forbids this. Only a priest has the power to read a person in an attempt to remove the eye. You must, instead, ward off

the evil eye before it can affect you. To do this you can paint an eye in the middle of a blue charm, then wear it as a necklace or bracelet. People who have blue eyes are thought to be exceptional givers of the evil eye. For decades, Greeks were wary of compliments from Frank Sinatra.

WHEN AND WHERE TO SPIT

- If Greeks hear bad news they will spit on themselves three times to ward off the possibility of anything bad happening to them.

- Greek fishermen spit into their nets to ward off any evil likely to prevent them from getting a good catch.

- When a child is baptized, the priest will blow into the air three times to glorify the Trinity, and spit into the ground three times at the devil.

HOW TO BE GREEK . . .
ON THE DANCEFLOOR

When you go to a British party, it's the women who dance. The men skulk in the kitchen and talk about cars and football.

At a Greek party, it's the men who hit the dancefloor. The Greeks invented Country & Western, so it's no accident that their songs focus on two fundamental themes: 'You done me wrong' or 'Nobody knows the trouble I've seen'. The rule of thumb is pretty much that if you play a Greek song backwards, you get your woman back, your fishing boat back, and finally your donkey.

One by one, each man takes his turn to act out, with the most extravagant looks and gestures, his yearning for the one true love he'll never find again – or, if his wife is in the room, some other tragedy from his past.

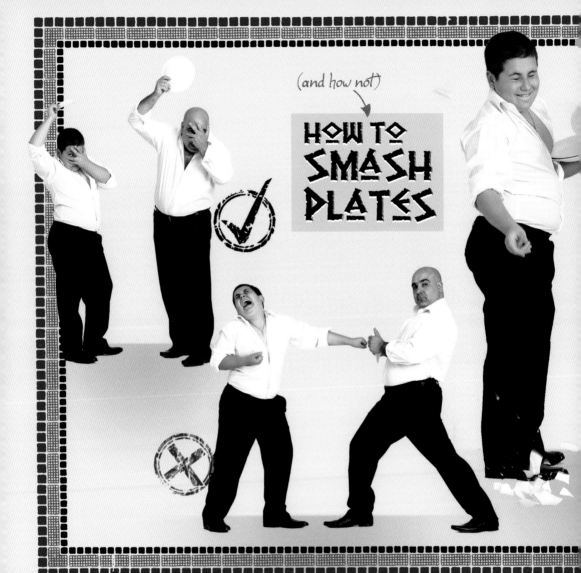

Getting Smashed

Back in the British kitchen, the chat about motors and the 'friendly' with Holland grinds to a halt as the boys get quietly smashed. In Greece, the plates get smashed – and not even a little bit quietly.

When a Greek listens to music, he gets so passionate he beats his chest and gives voice to the eternal question: 'What can I do?' The answer is simple. At this point in the evening, only the crash of a breaking plate can truly express the agony of men. There is nothing else on earth (nothing legal) which brings you quite the same release as hurling a plate to the floor. And another, and another. And on a really big night out, you can always call the owner over and ask, 'How much for the table?'

He'll say, 'Five hundred pounds.' Then he'll say, 'Cash.'

You will remove your wad of notes (which you keep in your hip pocket for just such an occasion), flip the table and *kalinihta* the lot.

They're Playing My Tune

Every Greek has a favourite song. You think it was written just for you. You lose yourself for the duration in the magic of the words and the swelling emotion of the music. A Greek's favourite song seizes the heart, and will only let it go when there are no more plates to smash.

A Greek singer sings about how we all want to live our lives. It's about the quest for perfection, the search for paradise with fishing boats in the foreground and the sun setting over the Aegean. We're always grappling with the Meaning of Life, always looking for happiness. But there is something we must not forget; something that lies at the heart of the old Cypriot tale my granddad used to tell me several times a day . . .

Every Greek has a favourite song. You think it was written just for you.

THE CURIOUS CASE OF THE FISHERMAN AND THE DOWN-TIME

A boat docked in a tiny Greek village. An American tourist complimented the fisherman on the quality of his catch and asked how long it took to fill his nets.

'Not very long,' *answered the Greek.*

'So why didn't you stay out longer?' *asked the American.* **'And catch more?'**

The Greek explained that what he had was sufficient to meet his needs and those of his family.

The American said, **'But what do you do with the rest of your time?'**

'I sleep late, play with my children, fish a little and take a siesta with my wife. In the evenings, I go into the village to see my friends, have a few drinks, play the guitar, sing a few songs . . . I have a full life.'

The American said, **'I have an MBA from Harvard and I can help you! You should start by fishing longer every day. You can then sell the extra fish you catch.**

'With the extra revenue, you can buy a bigger boat. With the extra money the larger boat will bring, you can buy a second and a third, and so on until you have an entire fleet.

'Instead of selling your fish to a middleman, you can negotiate directly with the processing plants and maybe even open your own plant. You can then leave this little village and move to Athens, London, or even New York! From there you can direct your global fishing empire.'

'How long would that take?' asked the Greek.

'Twenty, perhaps twenty-five years,' replied the American.

'And after that?'

'Afterwards? That's when it gets really interesting,' answered the American, laughing. 'When your business gets really big, you can start selling stocks and make billions!'

'Billions? Really? And after that?'

'After that you'll be able to retire, live in a tiny village near the coast, sleep late, play with your children, catch a few fish, take a siesta, and spend your evenings drinking and enjoying your friends . . .'

RESTAURANT

FRONT-OF-HOUSE

(a little bit)

HOW TO BE GREEK . . .
AT BUYING A RESTAURANT

There comes a moment in every Greek's life when, sooner or later, he's hit by the irresistible urge to stop just eating in *tavernas* and to buy one.

For most Greeks, the move into ownership makes solid sense – largely because most Greeks find it impossible to work for anybody but themselves. You couldn't imagine Jeremy Clarkson as assistant manager at your local Boots, could you, or Simon Cowell in charge of a BT customer-call centre? Like almost all the Greeks I know, they're simply too opinionated to hold down a conventional job.

The Importance of a Business Background

Probably the best business for a Greek is running a *taverna*. There's just you front-of-house, and the chef and a waitress – and if you play your cards right, your wife doubles up on the last two. This is not an imposition. Women spend a lot of time doing this stuff anyway, and they wouldn't do it if they didn't enjoy it. Why not allow them the luxury of a bit more time at the stove, or the chance to clear away the plates in the restaurant when they've finished at home?

Business Gods

The Ancient Greeks were the first to have a god of business. They called him Hermes because of his expensive scarves. And like the god Hermes, when I ran my restaurant my business methods were mythical – though I think the word the VAT man used was impenetrable. Anyway, the less said about the VAT people the better. Suffice to say, Archimedes wasn't the only one to turn the screw.

> *Probably the best business for a Greek is running a taverna*

RESTAURANT FRONT-OF-HOUSE

STEP 1: BUYING THE DREAM

I was twenty-four and didn't have a clue what I wanted to do with my life. I needed new challenges. After two years at catering college, I was the chairman and CEO of a highly successful car valeting company. It was me, the sponge and the bucket, and we were our own boss. We would get up when we wanted, work when we wanted, and go home and watch Al Pacino videos when we wanted.

Colman's made their fortune from the mustard left on the side of the plate, and it was like that with my empire. I would tell people they were getting a valet with a special wax that would keep their bodywork clean until the precise moment I saw them again the same time next week. The wax was Fairy Liquid, but for fifteen quid and twenty minutes' work, what could they expect?

I walked past a Greek restaurant every day on the way to my office in Morrison's car park.

One day, and don't ask me why, I stopped. I walked in and said to the owner, 'Any chance of you ever selling this?'

He said, 'I'm amazed you should ask that – I'm just about to put it up for sale.'

'Really? How much do you want for it?'

'Eighty thousand.'

'Eighty thousand?!'

'How much have you got?'

'I haven't got anything.'

'See what you can raise, and then come back to me.'

I scraped together twenty-four grand from all over – by which I mean mostly from all over the underside of Granddad's mattress.

I went back to the restaurant, and the owner accepted it as a down-payment. The rest of the eighty grand, he lent me.

STEP 2: THE CUSTOMER IS ALWAYS RIGHT

When customers complain, it's very important that you listen carefully. Then file the experience away in the place you keep your parking tickets, and hope you never have to dig it out again.

We could nearly always deal with comments about the food with a bit of a laugh. The customers would be laughing so much about what they'd been given to eat that they couldn't really find it in themselves to complain. And we always pointed them in the direction of a nice place to eat on their way home.

There's an exception to every rule, of course, and one night I met the entire family . . .

HOW TO BE GREEK . . . WITH COMPLAINTS

It was the daughter's sixteenth birthday and they'd been having a brilliant night. We treated them like gold. Well, fake onyx, at least. The mother had brought a cake in earlier. I tucked the box away in the kitchen, and when the moment came we lit the candles and wheeled it out with all the staff singing 'Happy Birthday'.

At the end of the night, the father and daughter came up and thanked me, and the mother went overboard. 'Absolutely fantastic! I've never, ever had such a good time. You've made our night unbelievable.'

Little did I know that's what they were about to make mine.

As he paid the bill, the dad kept saying, 'Thank you so much, my daughter's had a really good time.'

I kept replying, 'Oh brilliant, thanks.'

The mum said, 'You couldn't go and put the remains of the cake in the box, could you?'

> **When the going gets tough, the tough get going to the kitchen**

'Of course,' I smiled. 'No problem.'

I went into the kitchen, picked up the cake, and looked around for the box. I couldn't see it anywhere. Somebody must have chucked it away. So I put the cake down, went back out, and they were all standing there – the mother, the father, the boyfriend and the birthday girl.

'You'll never guess what,' I laughed. 'They've thrown the cake box away. But never mind, I'll—'

Mum's jaw dropped. Her face was thunder. 'You what?'

'Somebody's thrown the cake box away. Never mind, I've got the cake, so what I'll do is, I'll—'

'I'm sorry . . . Did you just say somebody threw the cake box away?'

'Yes. But what I'll do, I'll make you a—'

'No, no, no – I don't quite believe what you're saying.'

'Sorry?'

'Somebody threw the cake box away?'

'Yeah, somebody threw the cake box away.' I was still laughing. 'Not the cake – I've got the cake – it's just the box . . .'

'I just don't believe this. This is disgusting. You've ruined our whole night.'

'The box! Not the cake, the box!'

'I know, the box – you've thrown the box away.'

At this point the dad weighed in. 'Oh my God!' He said it like he'd caught me goosing his wife. 'I do not believe this!'

And the boyfriend's gone, 'I'll just get the boys, shall I?'

I looked around. The restaurant was empty apart from them and one other table. 'What boys? You're not listening. It's not the cake, it's the very ordinary cardboard box.'

'I know very well what it is,' the mum wailed. 'I can't believe you've thrown it away. You've ruined her birthday.'

Now everyone's coming over. All the girlfriends and friends of the friends, and they've cornered me. Even if you're just a little bit Greek, you don't like to be cornered.

'Look, what can I do? I'm so sorry. If I'd have known . . . I think it was the washer upper . . . I'll kill him, shall I? It's a box, it's a cardboard cake box!'

'I don't think you're taking this seriously.'

'I know what – I'll make you a box.'

The dad glared at me like I'd added his daughter to the goosing list. 'I think you should make it up to us . . .'

Aha! Here we go. So that's what it's all about . . .

'Oh right – so how do you think I should make it up to you?'

'I think you should take something off the bill.'

They all crowded round.

'How much do you think a cardboard cake box is worth?'

'Maybe ten quid a head.'

Getting Your Just Desserts

Just to get rid of them, I took a hundred quid off the bill, went back to the kitchen to fetch the cake, and walked them to the door.

Another customer was just about to go. He leant right across the dad to shake my hand. 'Mate,' he said. 'A blinding night, an absolute blinding night. It's a shame you get plonkers like this trying to ruin it for everyone.'

The dad froze. The boyfriend looked around.

'No need to fetch the boys,' I said. 'Just go.'

They melted through the door, a hundred quid better off than they should have been.

My new friend said, 'Lucky he left, mate. I would have had him.'

'Don't worry,' I said. 'What goes around, comes around.'

And so it would. The great big wheel of karma would come full circle as soon as they tucked into the remains of the cake.

You see, by the time the cake came back out of the kitchen door there was a whole lot more Greek in it than there had been when it went in.

AND THEN, OF COURSE, THERE'S THE GREEK WAY OF COMPLAINING. 'WHAT DO YOU MEAN, THERE'S SOME CAKE LEFT?!'

RESTAURANT FRONT-OF-HOUSE

(a little bit)

HOW TO BE GREEK . . .
ON OPENING NIGHT

We'd been planning and planning the opening day for ages, and most of the work went into the guest list. Whittling numbers for any occasion down to three figures is one of the hardest things for a Greek to do.

I said to my brother, 'Let's do a buffet.'

He said, 'Are you mad? We can't do a buffet. We've got important people coming. They'll expect à la carte.'

We argued, and compromises were made. A la carte it would be.

We hired an Egyptian chef. He told me he worked at the Hilton, and that was me impressed. I bought a beautiful suit, and everything was ready. Come the night – disaster. At least half the guests were Brits and arrived at 7.30 on the dot. The waiters were friends, helping me out for free. They looked the business in black trousers and crisp white shirts. It was just a pity they didn't have a clue what they were doing.

I ran around meeting and greeting and taking a hundred simultaneous orders, and thought everything was going well. But as the night wore on, I couldn't help noticing there was no food out.

I finally got a tap on the shoulder and somebody said, 'You'd better come into the kitchen.'

'What's the matter?'

'Just come.'

Hell's Kitchen

Dockets were lined up the length of the hot plate, and the chef was frozen to the spot in front of them. All he could do was stare.

'What's going on? Can't you cope? You said you worked in the Hilton.'

'In the Hilton all the orders don't come in at once.'

A reasonable point. I looked around for my brother. I couldn't see him anywhere. I knew he'd slipped off into the restaurant, well away from me.

I looked up at the ceiling and took a deep breath. I said, 'Please, God, if you love me, open the ground and take me now.'

It was the worst moment of my life.

All the Top Chefs Improvise

I took a deep breath and considered my options. It didn't take long. Suicide seemed like a good one.

One of the most traditional of Greek dishes is *kleftiko*. The demands of the situation had required us to improvise a little and move away from three thousand years of tradition. We had entombed it in filo pastry and called it Lamb Tutankhamen. Predictably, it was a catastrophe. You picked it up and the meat dropped out.

Then, from somewhere, came a burst of inspiration. I ripped all the dockets off the hot plate and threw them in the bin. I rolled up my sleeves and together we grilled everything we could lay our hands on. And when it had turned brown, we threw it onto every available plate.

When there was nothing left to grill, I put my suit back on and went back to face the guests.

I walked out to deafening silence. Not a single guest had got what they'd ordered.

I sat down at one of my friend's tables.

RESTAURANT FRONT-OF-HOUSE

There was this one plonker I'd only invited so I could show off. I didn't even like him. He – of all people – stood up and proposed a toast. 'Ladies and gentlemen, Demi has made the worst mistake of his life. Let's hope he can find a way to rectify it.'

I laid my head on the table and started to cry. To be (a little bit) Greek is to be (a little bit) emotional, but this was off the scale. I bawled.

Then something amazing happened. People started to come over and pat me on the back. Many of them were waiters. 'How much?' they asked. 'People want their bills.'

From under my arm I went, 'Forget it. They don't have to pay. It's free.'

And do you know what? We made more money that night than on any night since. People were too embarrassed to come and say goodnight. Instead, they just emptied their wallets.

There were many lessons to be learned from the experience. And if I hadn't been Greek, I might have done so.

(a little bit)

HOW TO BE GREEK . . .
ABOUT DRUGS

One of the great bonuses of being a Greek is how much money you save on illegal substances. The only recreational chemicals my granddad ever used went by the street names of Black Label and King Edward Invincibles, and what was good enough for that Greek god is good enough for me.

One of my suppliers at the restaurant one time was called Darryl. That tells you something about him straight away; as far as I'm aware there's never been a St Darryl – so no way was he of the Greek persuasion. Darryl, a skinny little chap, would come by every week and deliver food and I never once questioned his bills. One week I'd go, 'How much do I owe you?'

'Two hundred and fifty.'

'Well, here's two thirty, it's all I've got on me.'

The week after it was 320, and 400 soon after that. I didn't pay it all, but I came pretty close.

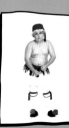

Do you notice anything about the cost curve? I didn't. I just used to think: blimey, do we really go through that much with the restaurant only open two nights a week? But every time I thought it, he would put an arm around me and say, 'Demetri! My friend! How you doing?' and before I knew it we were back outside at his van, laughing and joking, and I was peeling notes from my wad like there was no tomorrow.

This went on for months, until one week someone else came by. An elderly woman. She goes, 'Your order is here, and here's your bill.'

I looked at the bill. £60. 'Where's Darryl?'

She said, 'I'm Darryl's mum. We've had a bit of trouble with him. He's in rehab.'

'Oh dear – what for?'

'An expensive habit.'

'You're kidding?'

'I wish I was. He's been taking cocaine. We've only just found out. We've no idea where he's been getting the money.'

'That's terrible,' I said. 'Look, here's forty, it's all I've got on me.'

(a little bit)

HOW TO BE GREEK . . .
WITH THE TAX MAN

If there's one thing I've learnt from my lifetime as a Greek it's this: you can't win the lottery if you haven't bought a ticket. And here's another: if a man from the Inland Revenue phones and says he's popping round, make sure you've kept your receipts.

Think of all the great Greek entrepreneurs, such as Ari Onassis, Stavi Niarchos, Ricky Branson. They weren't just touched by the hand of fate – though whoever knitted Ricky's jumpers was definitely touched in some way. None of them woke up in the morning, rubbed on some Zivania and nipped off to buy another ship, or, in Ricky's case, spaceship. Good fortune didn't just fall off the back of a donkey straight into their pockets.

> *The harder you work at being a little bit Greek, the luckier you'll become*

Greeks don't really believe in destiny these days, which is probably why we invented the Midas touch. We make our own luck. And when the taxman visits, you need it in spades.

When I managed (and I use the term loosely) the restaurant, I found it hard enough keeping my head in order, let alone the paperwork. The Greek approach to financial matters is to round the figures up or down until they feel more or less right – the government do it all the time, and even though he's a long way from being even a tiny bit Greek, what's good enough for Gordon Brown is good enough for me.

A Tax Inspector Calls

I'd been at the helm of my restaurant for about six years when the tax people rang to say they'd like to come round.

'Certainly,' I said. 'Table for how many?'

It seemed I hadn't heard right. They weren't coming for the *souvlaki* – though I got the feeling that when the time came to explain my financial systems they might find themselves in for a bit of cabaret.

I have to admit, the phone call was a bolt from the blue. I didn't think these sorts of people knew where I worked. I didn't think they even knew I existed. I mean, I'd never replied to any of their letters or anything, or been a bother to them in any way. Good citizenship is important to a Greek.

'Could you have your books and accounts ready, Mr Demetriou?'

Could I? Good question. I employed one of my friends' dads as a book-keeper. He wasn't a real book-keeper, but he was cheap. He worked for a timber company in their book-keeping department, so I thought he knew what he was doing. He might have done, if only I'd let him get on with it. The problem was, I ran the business how I wanted to run it. The only overhead I kept under a tight rein was ink for his pens and ledgers to use it in.

Small Brown Envelopes

Cash is king, in all walks of Greek life. I'd kept faithful records, it's just that they weren't exactly in the form that others expected. But that's the Greek way. See something and improve on it. When it came to innovation, I couldn't see the difference between bookkeeping and shipbuilding.

When they arrived, I handed over my receipts in a Tescos bag. Greeks always shop at Tescos whenever they can. It's a Greek firm, and we like to look after our own.

I also gave them the books, and my friend's dad was beside me. They didn't ask either of us any questions. And everyone was really smiley. I thought: how good is this? They've not done anything, they've not said anything. They're not as bad as everyone makes out. I got a bit carried away and offered all kinds of information I probably should have kept to myself, but they were nice people and we were having a good time.

When they'd left, I turned to my book-keeper and said, 'Didn't that go well?'

'Yeah,' he went. 'To be honest, really, really well.'

I said, 'How does that compare with other visits?'

He said, 'I don't know.'

'What do you mean, you don't know?'

'That's the first time I've ever seen a taxman.'

'You've never seen a taxman?'

'No, never. The accountants do that.'

It Never Rains But It Pours

A few weeks later, I got another phone call. 'Mr Demetriou, can you please be available at eleven o'clock. We'd like to see you again.'

'No problem, I'll be here. What's it about?'

I thought they'd have gone through the Tescos bag by now and concluded I was due a rebate.

She went, 'Don't worry, we'll talk about it when I get there.'

The two of them walked in at 11 o'clock on the dot, so that answered one question. The Inland Revenue didn't match inspectors to customers. They couldn't possibly have been Greek.

They'd brought back the bag though, which was nice of them.

'How have you been, Mr Demetriou?' the woman asked.

'Really good.'

'How's business?'

'Not so good. Not very busy at all.'

Her friend, who hadn't said a word up to this point, picked up the bag and emptied it on the table.

'Mr Demetriou, these are all the receipts that you gave us.'

I looked at them. 'You're right.'

He fished in his pocket. 'And here's a copy of a receipt from one of our investigators.'

'Investigators?'

'Yes, we sent a gentleman to eat in your restaurant. He paid cash. Here's the copy of the receipt. Where's the original?'

'What do you mean, where's the original?'

He said, 'Well, in there somewhere should be the top copy of his receipt. Can you find it for us?'

I went, 'How am I meant to find it? What do you want me to do, look through these receipts?'

'That's precisely what I want you to do, Mr Demetriou. It must be in there somewhere, because here's the copy.'

I looked at the pile again. 'How am I going to find it in there?'

He smiled smugly. 'You can't find it because it's not there.'

I got the distinct feeling that whatever was coming my way it wasn't a rebate.

'Therefore, Mr Demetriou, I can now tell you that you're under investigation for tax evasion, and it can be punishable by up to six years' imprisonment. Have you got anything to say?'

I leant forward and put my head in my arms and I started crying. I went, 'No, I've got nothing to say, why are you doing this to me? I've done nothing wrong.'

He said, 'I think you'll find you have. You're under investigation and we'll be forwarding you our findings.'

I was still crying. 'Thank you very much.'

They were leaving and I was still crying and thanking them.

The woman put a hand on my shoulder and said, 'If I was you I'd find myself a good accountant.'

I went, 'OK, no problem. Thank you very much.'

In the Lap of the Gods and Bean-counters

I went home, and it was another one of those moments where I thought: please God, open up the ground and take me now. My son had just been born and now he'd be fatherless for six years, maybe only three if I was let off for good behaviour.

One of my friends told me of a company up in London that specialized in this sort of thing. I called them up and the guy I spoke to said, 'Mr Demetriou, would you please bring £3,000 cash with you. We can't accept cheques because you're under investigation for tax evasion. We need to know that you've got enough money to cover our first instalment.'

I got on the tube with the restaurant books under my arm and three grand in my pocket. I went up to these beautiful offices in the City and sat in reception. A lady came and took me upstairs to a huge wood-panelled boardroom. The first thing she asked me was, 'Mr Demetriou, have you brought the retainer?'

'No problem.' I handed her the wad.

She called someone to come and count the £3,000 and wrote me a

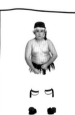

receipt. Not just any receipt; this was really elegant and everything like that, with real fountain pen ink.

The lady came back in, and opened the books. After about fifteen minutes she said, 'Mr Demetriou, it doesn't take a genius to figure out that you are in a lot of trouble. I'm afraid to say they really have got you.'

I went, 'Is that it?'

She said, 'I'm afraid your bookkeeping system is far from orthodox.'

'Orthodox? What do you mean? Why are you bringing the church into this all of a sudden?

She shook her head. 'You know this offence is punishable by up to six years?'

'That's what the tax people said! Is that the best you can do?'

She said, 'What would you like me to do? You are in a lot of trouble.'

I felt those tears welling up again.

'Can I have my money back, please? I'll go somewhere else.'

'OK.'

The bloke came back in, counted the money out again, took the receipt off me and gave me the money back. I put it in the same envelope that I'd brought it in, and then I left. As I walked back to the tube all I could think was, 'I'm stuffed.'

I'd tried to improve the world's financial systems and I'd failed. What was I going to do?

A Bird in the Hand
Is Worth Two in Shepherds Bush

Luckily – and it's funny how often that word crops up when you're Greek – a friend of my wife's had the answer. I was talking about it and she said, 'Oh, my husband's an accountant.'

'Let me guess – he works for a timber company?'

'No, he's got his own business in Shepherds Bush. Why don't you go and see him?'

I did just that, and this guy, I'll be completely honest with you, he looked like he didn't know what he was doing. I didn't get a good feeling about him at all. But what did I know? I'd thought the book-keeper must be brilliant because he had leather patches on the elbows of his jumper. At least this one didn't want three grand up front.

152

He wrote the Inland Revenue a letter and told me not to worry.

'That's all very well,' I said, 'but everyone else is saying I'm in the shit.'

'No, no, no, don't worry. I deal with this sort of thing all the time.'

I couldn't believe it. Every man and his dog's on my case, and this guy's telling me not to worry.

But do you know what? To this day – and it's been a few years now – I haven't heard a dickie bird from the tax people. I don't know what he did to get me out of trouble, but whatever it was, he must have been really good. It makes me think sometimes I must have someone looking after me. I feel almost blessed.

Sometimes good luck falls off the back of a donkey . . .

RESTAURANT
KITCHEN NIGHTMARES

(a little bit)

HOW TO BE GREEK . . .
ABOUT RECYCLING

When he cooked in my uncle's restaurant, I often sampled Granddad's *moussaka* – and it never tasted quite right.

'Granddad, there's something not quite right with this *moussaka*.'

'No, no, it's fine.'

There weren't that many Greeks in North Cheam. The Brits who flocked to the restaurant probably thought it was supposed to taste of old socks.

'How old is the milk?'

'A few days. There's cheese in there. You won't know the difference.' He didn't even blush.

Renew. Reuse. Recycle. That was Papou's mantra long before Alexis Gore found the hole in the ozone layer.

He believed in never throwing anything away, which was just as well for my nan.

HOW TO BE GREEK . . .
ABOUT HEALTH & SAFETY

Papou would come up some afternoons and sit with me. One day we were laying out the tables for the weekend and a group of about fifteen people stopped outside and studied the menu.

This guy comes in and asks, 'Are you open for lunch?'

'No, not really.'

Granddad was straight on the case. 'Tell him to come in.'

'We've got no chef.'

'What do you mean, we've got no chef?' He banged his chest. 'I will cook!'

I waved them in. They looked like tourists. Goodness knows what tourists were doing in Cockfosters. Maybe they were lost.

They settled down at a long table and I followed Papou into the kitchen.

'What are we going to cook for them?'

'Do them some dips to start, and tell them –' he opened the big fridge and saw the skewers the chef had prepared for the weekend '– tell them we'll do them some nice kebabs.'

A Taste of the Old Country

I told the customers we could do a set menu, dips and kebabs, and they seemed to like the idea. I went back to the kitchen and spooned out potato salad, *taramosalata* and *tsatziki*. Granddad, meanwhile, had fired up the charcoal and started warming the pitta bread.

I served the *meze* and went back to the kitchen once more. Granddad had a fistful of kebab skewers at the ready, and a bottle of beer. This was obviously thirsty work.

He took a swig, threw back his head like a fire-eater and covered the kebabs with a fine spray of Heineken. He must have thought it really did refresh the parts other beers cannot reach.

'Papou – what are you doing?'

'It makes them taste nicer.'

'Can't you just pour it?'

'No, no.' He looked surprised. 'It's the traditional way.'

I had a series of alarming flashbacks to my uncle's restaurant in North Cheam. I thought of the number of people in those ten years who must have eaten my granddad's cooking . . . and probably thought the meat was supposed to taste of lager and Rothmans.

And to think of the number of times he'd slagged off my staff. They were never good enough. Papou not only had a PhD in I Told You So, he invented the course and built the university. 'Such a shame you never learned to cook from me. Such a shame, you getting ripped off by your chefs because you can't cook yourself because you never let me teach you.'

I certainly hadn't seen his own special version of a spit roast.

MARINADED BEER KEBABS

Ingredients
4kg lamb – large chunks
1 bottle of beer

Method
- Prepare your coal BBQ.
- Load large skewers with big chunks of lamb.
- To marinade; take a large swig of beer, hold in mouth to attain optimum heat then spray, in a fire-eater sort of way, the entire length of each kebab.
- Once fully saturated, the kebabs can be placed on the BBQ and cooked until evenly browned.

(a little bit)

HOW TO BE GREEK . . .
ABOUT COST-CUTTING

I don't recommend that you set out with the intention of serving terrible food in your restaurant. I never did; that was just the way the cookie crumbled. Or in my case, the meringue base.

We weren't great at making desserts. Come to think of it, we weren't great at making starters or mains either. We ended up buying really fancy things like big cheesecakes and trays of *baklava*, but even they got left. People were more interested in standing up to watch the cabaret or dancing on their chairs and tables.

I suddenly saw a way of cutting a bit of a corner.

Every Little Helps

I looked around Tescos. I saw brandy-snap cases, which the customers would have gone for, but they were a bit expensive. And then I saw meringue bases. They were so cheap – just pennies each. I piled a trolley

> **We weren't great at making desserts . . . or starters or mains either**

high with them, and another with forty or fifty cans of squirty cream – and a few tubs of my secret ingredient.

That night, just before the dessert service, I spread the bases out over the work surface and ran round squirting a dollop of cream in each. Then I stood at one end and opened a tub of my secret ingredient. Gripping it in my hand, I threw my arm out like I was casting a net, and the hundreds-and-thousands rained down.

The waiters were standing by. This was a finely tuned operation. Every minute counted. In fact, the customers had just seven in which to eat the things before the cream turned to liquid and the hundreds-and-thousands dissolved in the mush.

SPECIAL GREEK DESSERT

Ingredients
50 meringue nests
2 cans squirty cream
1 tub hundreds-and-thousands

Method
Line up meringue nests. Run along with cans, squirting dollop of cream in each. When complete, stand back, open tub of hundreds-and-thousands and, like a Greek god, rain the speckles down. Serve at once before it all turns to mush.

Three Michelin Stars

Night after night, I thought for sure that somebody was going to come and complain, but they never did. Nobody said a word. Why should they? The desserts were as bad as the main courses. The only decent things on the table were the starters. Until, that is, I heard the chef complaining to the waiters one day. 'We're on the main course for table ten, and table six has just walked in and wants pitta bread. Where am I going to cook the pitta bread?'

'Can't you cook it in advance?' I asked.

'No, it has to be hot.'

Stuff the pitta bread then, I thought – and not with slivers of kebab meat. We bought in loaves of ordinary bread and cut them into chunks. I'd finally achieved the full three Michelin stars in reverse: we were the only Greek restaurant in the whole of England that didn't serve pitta bread, and every one of our courses was crap.

(a little bit)

HOW TO BE GREEK . . .
ABOUT IRISH DANCING

If you've followed my instructions to the letter, chances are the food at your restaurant is so terrible you're going to have to come up with something to divert the customers' attention from it, and sharpish.

Our cabaret night started as an hour's worth of running around and making people laugh to take their minds off their indigestion. Before we knew it, we were playing to packed houses.

We began to get a lot of hen parties coming in. One night there were 140 women at the tables, and the five or six terrified waiters were the only men in sight. I went into the kitchen and pulled out my address book. 'You've got to come over,' I said to every man who answered. 'And bring your dancing shoes.'

'What about my kilt?' one of my cousins joked.

Why not, I said, and I only discovered later that this was no ordinary kilt. Sewn inside, hidden from view, was a great big plastic thingy.

HOW TO IRISH DANCE

(Greek)

Wilkommen, Bienvenue, Parakalo

We blindfolded the bride-to-be, and sat her facing the dancefloor. Out came my cousin in his kilt, and he danced to the Pogues. He gyrated in front of her, told a few jokes and announced it was time for the karaoke to begin.

But first we lifted the blindfold and he lifted his kilt – to reveal the Colossus of Rhodes.

She loved it, and so did her 139 mates. They loved the night, they loved the restaurant and they loved the owner – if only because I promised them the thingy was modelled on my own.

The following week, I was at home watching the telly and minding my own business. A film about *Riverdance* came on, and I watched, transfixed. Michael Thingummy was good, but I could see plenty of room for improvement. What Greek wouldn't have?

I practised and practised, and two days later, I made my debut.

The rest, as they say, is a little bit of Greek history.

The Greeks don't do Irish dancing, but if they did, it would probably be the best Irish dancing in the world.

Probably the best Lagi in the world